IMAGES
of America

LEVITTOWN
THE FIRST 50 YEARS

IMAGES
of America

LEVITTOWN
THE FIRST 50 YEARS

Margaret Lundrigan Ferrer and Tova Navarra

ARCADIA

First published 1997
Copyright © Margaret Lundrigan Ferrer and Tova Navarra, 1997

ISBN 0-7524-0465-2

Published by Arcadia Publishing,
an imprint of the Chalford Publishing Corporation
One Washington Center, Dover, New Hampshire 03820
Printed in Great Britain

Library of Congress Cataloging-in-Publication Data applied for

To my dearest friend Tova and our "Larky Life"
—MLF

I dedicate this book to the late Cecile J. Roberts and Phil Heron,
and all shining examples of Levittowners who made monkeys of the critics
and fostered William Levitt's creative and enduring vision.
—TN

A potato harvest, in the early
1940s, on land that was to become
Levittown. (Courtesy of the
Nassau County Museum
Collection, Long Island Studies
Institute)

Contents

Acknowledgments

The authors extend very special thanks to the Levittown Public Library and its reference department—a wonderful example of the role local libraries fill as community centers for learning. We are indebted to librarians Janet Spar, for her unsurpassed assistance and support, the late Cecile Roberts, an original Levittowner who graciously shared reminiscences and photographs, and Ann Glorioso, who happily found files for us and the time to chat about her life in Levittown. Original Levittowners Jerry and Clare Worthing deserve much praise for their family photographs and perspectives. Joseph Ferlise, of Ferlise Photographers, and Thomas and Beth Dalton, of the Dalton Funeral Home, contributed excellent insights and snapshots. We are also extremely grateful to Dr. Barbara Kelly, of Hofstra University, and Dr. Mildred Murphy DeRiggi, of the Long Island Studies Institute and the Nassau County Museum, for their invaluable assistance. Thanks go also to Mary Heron Quinn, of Flowers by Phil (Heron), for wonderful anecdotes of early Levittown life; Lynne Matarrese, of the Levittown Historical Society, for pre-Levitt information; Jim Edmondson, of YOM; Polly Dwyer, of the St. Francis Episcopal Church; Pat Freund, a friendly Levittowner who provided contacts and information; E.H. "Gene" Rifkind, of the Willingboro Public Library, for his cheerful helping hand to unannounced visitors; George Douglas, of Levittown, Pa., for his "Country Clubber tour" and thoughtfulness; Billy Joel, one of America's finest singers and songwriters, for terrific family photos and Jane Arginteanu, of Maritime Music, Inc., who made Mr. Joel's contribution possible; Levittowner Donna Ryan, for digging into the family album; and Randall Gabrielan, a fellow Arcadia author, for his camaraderie and support. In addition to warm fuzzies to Sarah Maineri, Jim Burkinshaw, Michael Joseph Guillory, and the Arcadia staff, we would like to remember the late author Pam Conrad, whose children's book *Our House: Stories of Levittown* tickled many an imagination about life in the community created by a man who fought "City Hall" and won.

Introduction

"An invasion of armies can be resisted, but not an idea whose time has come."
—from *Histoire d'un Crime* (1852) by Victor Hugo

"Levittown was an experiment—THE experiment of the 1940s.
It tested the GI housing bill . . . mass production techniques . . .
and the American citizen's capacity for community leadership . . ."
—from an article "Levittown, B.L.-A.L. Before and After Levitt"
in *The Levittown Tribune* of June 12, 1969

To look out over the potato fields of Island Trees, Long Island, in 1946 was to see more than 1,200 acres of farmland devastated by a fancifully named parasite—the Golden Nematode. But when William Levitt looked out over this Nassau County land, located 32 miles east of Manhattan, he saw the solution to a housing disaster created by the multitude of GIs returning from service in World War II.

The "Henry Ford" of the housing industry, with bits of P.T. Barnum and the character George Bailey in the movie *It's a Wonderful Life* thrown in for good measure, Levitt would change the face of suburbia forever.

Did Levitt invent the suburb? Certainly not, considering that suburbs have existed for thousands of years, from the villas of medieval Italy, where aristocrats escaped the cities' heat and crowds, to respites like Versailles, a getaway just outside Paris that suited nobles who wanted a change of scenery for their wild doings. Levittown, New York, however, would become the quintessential "Everyman's" suburb of the mid-1900s. It was the average person's chance to acquire a piece of the American dream. From the struggling potato and vegetable farms of Island Trees, Levitt & Sons created the first of many Levitt communities in the United States and Europe.

William Jaird Levitt was nothing if not a visionary. He was born on February 11, 1907, the first of two sons of Abraham Levitt (a lawyer/contractor born in the Williamsburg section of Brooklyn) and his wife Pauline (Biederman). William seems to have always been on the move. *Esquire* magazine quotes him on his dropping out of New York University after his junior year: "I got itchy. I wanted to make a lot of money. I wanted a big car and lots of clothes." His father (1880–1962) founded Levitt and Sons building contractors in 1929. The entrepreneurial William was made president; his brother Alfred became vice-president and chief designer. After becoming disillusioned with the high overhead associated with the custom market, William investigated and embraced the advantages of mass production.

An officer during the war, Levitt put his time in Seabees to good use. One of the things he learned is that rules are often best broken. Here he orchestrated Levittown. He directed his brother, then a civilian, on the purchase of the land. He then orchestrated a strategy composed of financial support offered to GIs by the government (the Federal Housing Administration, or FHA, loans) and his ingenious means of adapting assembly-line techniques to home construction. With his plan aided and abetted by the Long Island Railroad and Robert Moses' system of highways, Levitt's natural showmanship enabled him to get his message to the people. The man whose favorite college motto was "The masses are asses" was destined to become known as "Everyone's Best Friend."

Levitt's story becomes juicier because of tremendous opposition and intrigue. His houses were denounced as "all made out of ticky-tacky and they all look just the same" in the American protest song "Little Boxes." They were declared incipient slums by writer Lewis Mumford, and called an incubator for moral atrophy and intellectual stagnation.

Of course, the not-necessarily-little "boxes" violated a long-held assumption about American homes: they had no basements. When the Hempstead building code on basements threatened to close down Levitt's construction, the former GIs responded en masse. They inundated the zoning board and local newspapers with 1,500 letters demanding construction. Levitt pushed aside moral indignation and housing codes and plunged further into his Magnum Opus. By 1947, approximately 2,000 "Capes," as a few of the models were called, were available for ex-GIs to rent. By 1951, 17,000 homes on a thousand lanes had been built.

For veterans who made it home from the war, the Levitt house, equipped with a Bendix washing machine and a waiting-to-be-finished attic, was similar to what ambitious folk acquired during the Gold Rush or a nineteenth-century land-grab. For the generation that produced the "Baby Boomers" and asked only for an opportunity to move out of overcrowded apartments and Quonset huts, Levittown was golden.

Today, a barometer of William Levitt's success comes forth through the words of a third-generation, Levittown, PA, man, George Douglas: "It was great to grow up in Levittown." Whatever one's point of view, the "ticky-tacky" houses set an uncanny dialogue in motion. In their small "fiefdom," the Levitts evoked feelings and treatment usually reserved for royalty. In his later years, William, the "uncrowned prince of Levittown," fell on hard times. Levitt sold his firm to International Telephone and Telegraph for $92 million. He reportedly lost a fortune in the 1970s and '80s as a result of unsuccessful business dealings. The man who once headed the largest construction company in New York was eventually barred from building in that state.

But Levitt often said he was more comfortable with the people of Levittown, where homes sold for less than $8,000, than he was with the muckety-mucks. In a videotaped, Hofstra University interview three weeks before his death, he said he would like to be remembered as "a guy that gave value for low-cost housing, not somebody who gave value for half-a-million dollar houses. Anybody could do that." Levitt died of kidney failure at age eighty-six on January 28, 1994. *The Levittown Tribune* of February 2, 1994, reported that he is survived by his third wife, Simone, of Upper Brookville, NY; two sons, James of Devon, PA, and William Jr. of California; and three stepdaughters, Nicole Bernstein of Manhattan, Denise Chernoff of Orlando, FL, and Gaby Altman of Princeton, NJ.

One story has it that Levitt, not known for his modesty, liked to tell of a little Levittown girl who said in her nightly prayers, "God bless Mommy, Daddy, and Mr. Levitt." Perhaps this makes the most fitting epitaph for William Levitt and his version of Utopia, which celebrates its 50th anniversary in October 1997.

One

Pre-Levitt

"The most striking thing about Levittown is the change . . . almost overnight . . .
from a countrified section into a virtual city. Four years ago,
it was just a potato field with a few houses. I liked it better then.
I like the country better than a crowded town."
—Mrs. Alfred Badolato, from a December 12, 1951 interview in the *Nassau Review-Star*

"When the decision is up before you—
and on my desk I have a motto which says, 'The buck stops here'—
the decision has to be made."
—Harry S Truman, December 19, 1952

Was there life B.L.—before Levitt? Some places are so tightly associated with, or even defined by, particular events or times that it is difficult to imagine how they were before—like Salem before the trials, Waterford before crystal, or Oxford before the university. But Levittown did have an engaging history before Levitt.

The area once known as Island Trees dates back to 1644, when Captain John Seaman and Robert Jackson purchased 1,500 acres from Native Americans and settled in the area with their families. Seaman and Jackson, both of whom had relocated from Stamford, Connecticut, were active in civic affairs. Their numerous descendants (Captain Seaman had eight sons and eight daughters; Jackson had two sons and two daughters) involved themselves in agriculture. The settlers, given their religious inclination, called their place Jerusalem, which became a meeting place for Long Island Quakers. The Seamans joined the Society of Friends, and one of the Seamans preached at the meetinghouse until 1875, when many members of the society began to move away.

Farming continued as a way of life into the nineteenth century. Long Island farmers provided much of the produce for New York and surrounding areas. Many of the farmers were German, which is revealed in their names: Dengler, Rowehl, Gaenger, Meyer, Sparke, and Streeseman, among others. In 1858, John Streeseman and J. Bulling founded the German Methodist Church. In her article "Jerusalem Remembered," Jeanne Lewis writes that until World War I, services and Sunday school were conducted in German.

Levittown entered one of its most glamorous eras when, from 1908 to 1910, it became the site of the grandstand and reviewing stand for the Vanderbilt Cup Raceway Parkway. A precursor to today's modern highway, the 23.3-mile parkway was the first road built exclusively for cars. The first section, completed in 1908, ran from Bethpage to East Meadow (9 miles) and was made of reinforced concrete. The races attracted the well-to-do, including the Vanderbilts, Fords, Whitneys and Guggenheims. The 1910 Sixth Vanderbilt Cup Race drew 300,000 spectators. In an effort to get a better view of the cars, the crowd would surge forward, with some people falling onto the raceway. During the 1910 race, twenty-two people were injured and three died. This tragedy resulted in the relocation of the races to Savannah, Georgia, in 1911.

Long-noted for its potato production, Island Trees enjoyed a peak production of 2 million bushels in 1919. (Courtesy of the Nassau County Museum Collection, Long Island Studies Institute)

BEFORE THE MERRY OLDSMOBILE. In 1906, Walter Christie rides in his Christie Car, a symbol of America's growing love affair with the auto. The early cars cost as much as $40,000, which today would buy a luxury car such as a Lexus (much admired by the authors of this book). (Courtesy of the Nassau County Museum Collection, Long Island Studies Institute)

WHAT PRICE HESPERUS? A man surveys a car wrecked in an accident. A speed of 60 miles per hour must have seemed fantastic and dangerous to spectators who were just emerging from the horse-drawn buggy days. (Courtesy of the Nassau County Museum Collection, Long Island Studies Institute)

ON YOUR MARK . . . The starting line of 1908 was also the finish line for the 23-mile course. George Robertson won a race consisting of eleven laps around the course in his #16 American Locomobile. (Courtesy of the Nassau County Museum Collection, Long Island Studies Institute)

. . . GET SET . . . People wait eagerly for the races to begin. (Courtesy of the Nassau County Museum Collection, Long Island Studies Institute)

GO! The grandstand at Vanderbilt Raceway was built for the Fourth Vanderbilt Cup Race. Located at Orchid and Skimmer Lanes, it provided seating for hundreds of people. (Courtesy of the Nassau County Museum Collection, Long Island Studies Institute)

ANTS OR NO ANTS, people found the area around the motor parkway ideal for picnics before the races. (Courtesy of the Nassau County Museum Collection, Long Island Studies Institute)

A BIRD'S-EYE VIEW of Wantagh, the future Levittown. Author and Hofstra University faculty member Dr. Barbara Kelly referred to the land as "underdeveloped." Anticipating the post-war housing need, Levitt bought 200 acres at $225 per acre, with the option to buy 200 more acres each year. The area remains unincorporated and spans 7.3 square miles, including East Meadow, Hicksville, Wantagh, Westbury, and Oyster Bay and Hempstead townships. (Courtesy of the Nassau County Museum Collection, Long Island Studies Institute)

Two

Levittown

"Despite the skeptics and the professional critics and the Communists,
we believe in Levittown, in its honesty and goodness.
What's more, we believe most of the tenants feel as we do . . .
We know there is no place like it in the Nation. We worked hard and long to get it started
and we expect to stay long with it. We're proud of Levittown.
We know it's the greatest job we've ever done."
—Abraham, William J., and Alfred S. Levitt, July 1948

"And the Lord God said to Abraham (Levitt), 'Let there be homes!'"
—Thomas Dalton, in *The Levittowner*

"The Levittown era was like Camelot—a time during which it was a high priority of the American government and people to house young families who had more energy than money," said Hofstra University's Dr. Barbara Kelly in a recent interview. "There was a recognition that good houses support good family values. Whatever their motives in that era, Americans rallied for working people and their children. It saddens me that both the government and some people have lost incentive for doing that for young people today."

Levittown's heyday was not without critics. One of the most severe was writer Lewis Mumford (1895–1990), who assessed Levittown as "an incipient slum." In his book *The Fifties*, David Halberstam quotes Mumford describing Levittown as "a multitude of uniform, unidentifiable houses, lined up inflexibly on uniform roads, in a treeless . . . waste, inhabited by people of the same class, the same income, the same age group, witnessing the same television performances, eating the same . . . foods, conforming in every outward and inward respect to a common mold manufactured in the same central metropolis. Thus the ultimate effect of suburban escape in our time is, ironically, a low-grade uniform environment from which escape is impossible."

Books and movies also lampooned and satirized Levittown. John Keats wrote in *The Crack in the Picture Window*: "For literally nothing down, you too can find a box of your own in the fresh-air slums . . . around the edges of American cities." Halberstam also notes that the original movie *Invasion of the Body Snatchers* centered on "the horror of being in the 'burbs . . . neighbors whose lives had so lost their distinctiveness that they could be taken over by alien vegetable pods *and no one would know the difference*."

Other criticism harbored far, far thornier issues, such as the covenant Levitt imposed upon the homeowners. The first homes were rented to white veterans only. By the time homes were being sold, and for the next twenty years, it was a Levitt policy that blacks or Asians could not buy in. Given the nation's tension over racial discrimination, Levitt's covenant rankled, and justifiably. It seemed even to negate the enormous good he did. In the early '50s, according to Halberstam, Levitt replied: "The Negroes in America are trying to do in 400 years what the Jews in the world have not wholly accomplished in 6,000 years. As a Jew I have no room in my mind or heart for racial prejudice. But . . . I have come to know that if we sell one house to a Negro family, then 90 or 95 percent of our white customers will not buy into the community. That is their attitude, not ours . . . As a company our position is simply this: We can solve a housing problem, or we can try to solve a racial problem but we cannot combine the two."

Despite the wonderful/horrible duality, for the original Levittowners—some would call them pioneers—living well was truly the best revenge. Singer/songwriter Billy Joel remembers being a little boy living in the Bronx when his mother told him they were moving to the "country"— to a Levitt home in Hicksville, Long Island. Apparently the "pioneers" cared more about survival—and later about acquiring phone service, completing college degrees, raising kids, improving the school system, and individualizing their homes—than they could afford to suffer social criticism.

HAPPY CAMPERS? World War II veterans spent the night outside the Levitt office to sign up for Levitt homes in 1947. A May 10, 1985 *Newsday* article quoted veteran Paul Widlitz, later a state Supreme Court Justice: "Like everybody else, we were living with parents. Then we had a child and we were desperate. We got on the first list. We were number 107." (Collection of the Levittown Public Library)

TAKING ORDERS. On August 15, 1949, sales representatives sold 650 Levitt homes to 1,500 buyers in five hours. William Levitt, seated at the first table, said, "It's even bigger than we thought." In an assembly-line procedure similar to Levitt's building techniques, buyers were organized into five lines and sent to three separate tables: at the first were five Levitt salesmen; at the next, clerk/typists; and at the third, FHA and Veterans Administration representatives. (Collection of the Levittown Public Library)

LAYING THE GROUNDWORK. Construction of Jurgen (Jerry) and Clare Worthing's ranch began in 1951 after he, as an ex-GI, and his family had lived in a rented Cape. Worthing took pictures as the house went up. (Collection of the Levittown Public Library)

OOH, SUCH NICE, WARM FLOORS! The radiant heating system and the main plumbing lines created one of the controversies concerning Levitt homes. Heated water passed through pipes encased in concrete. The slab construction also eliminated having to excavate for a basement. People feared the pipes might crack, but only a few Levitt homeowners have had any problems with the heating. (Collection of the Levittown Public Library)

SMILE! A prospective homeowner takes pictures during the preliminary stage of the home's construction. Levitt was known to have said that if the Ancient Romans didn't see the need for basements, why should he? (Collection of the Levittown Public Library)

SLAB, 1,500; BASEMENT, 0. Slab foundations were approved for construction when the Hempstead Town Board's building code that mandated basement foundations was defeated. On May 27, 1947, vets swamped the board with appeals to allow Levitt to build 2,000 cellarless homes. One vet said, "Cellar or no cellar doesn't mean anything to me or anyone else here. We want the houses." Veteran George Dittus added, "No cellar beats one room in an attic where you freeze to death for $45 a month." (Newsday, May 28, 1947) (Collection of the Levittown Public Library)

LEVITT'S "FACTORY IN THE FIELD." Henry Ford's car-manufacturing techniques applied well to builders. Identical piles of building materials deposited on each home site awaited crews with specific jobs to do. Although many think of Levitt as limited to archetypal Capes, ranches and upscale models on 60-by-100-foot lots sold for $7,990, with a choice of four different roof lines and including a Bendix washing machine, two-way fireplace, and built-in Admiral television. (Collection of the Levittown Public Library)

SEE YOU BACK AT THE RANCH. In addition to the archetypal Capes, the next phase of construction was upscale ranch models, answering the federal government's charge that the market for Capes had been saturated. (Collection of the Levittown Public Library)

DOWN WITH UNIONS. The worker on a tractor represents Levitt's opposition to union labor. He saw it as a system that protected the least productive workers at higher cost to everyone. Levitt did, however, give incentives for increased productivity, and many workers did well financially because of this system. (Collection of the Levittown Public Library)

UP ON THE ROOF. The Worthing ranch nears completion, thanks to the assembly-line system and adept workers who each had a specialty. While some exclusively did framing or tile bathrooms, others devoted their efforts to installing kitchen cabinets, and so forth. The result? Greater productivity and lower costs. (Collection of the Levittown Public Library)

MORE CEMENT, I SAY! A cement truck operates on the Levitt homesites. (Collection of the Levittown Public Library)

ON THE LEVEL . . . Workers level the ground to prepare for building and landscaping. At the height of production, workers were completing thirty-six homes a day. (Collection of the Levittown Public Library)

AND DOWN THE STREET. Street-paving was part of Levitt's "big picture." The paved roads became Weaving, Bluegrass, Shelter, and hundreds of other unusually named lanes characteristic of Levittown—"The Town of a Thousand Lanes." (Collection of the Levittown Public Library)

MODEL CONSTRUCTION. Thomas Dalton, owner of a funeral business in Levittown, also published a small paper called *The Levittowner*, which elicited an archive of photographs such as this one. Interestingly, Levitt modeled his building techniques on those of Henry Ford, who died on April 7, 1947, a few months before the construction of Levitt homes began. (Courtesy of Thomas and Beth Dalton)

FIRST COME, FIRST SERVED. This $7,900 ranch proved a positive step for struggling young families. Levitt vehemently opposed middlemen, closing, and any additional costs and did everything he could to eliminate them. You paid $7,900, period. Still, Levitt testified before a Congressional subcommittee, "If we could buy directly from the manufacturer, we could sell a $7500 house for $5000." (Courtesy of Thomas and Beth Dalton)

COME AND GET 'EM. This 1950 ad displays the four styles of ranches available. An ad in *The New York Times* read: "This is Levittown! All yours for $58. You're a lucky man, Mr. Veteran. Uncle Sam and the world's largest builder have made it possible for you to live in a charming house in a delightful community without having to pay for them with your eyeteeth." (Collection of the Levittown Public Library)

THE IDEAL PICTURE. An aerial-view drawing of the Levitt Model Home Site on Hempstead Turnpike. (Collection of the Levittown Public Library)

FOR ART'S SAKE. This drawing shows a 1947–48 Cape Cod design. Although he not did formally study architecture, Alfred Levitt had considerable talent. He created a home of only 750 square feet, with a design that maximized the use of space and included an easily expandable attic. Even Lewis Mumford acknowledged Levitt's design as superior to other similarly priced homes. (Collection of the Levittown Public Library)

JUST YOUR TYPE—A TYPE 5 CAPE. Said Alfred Levitt in the March 1949 *Architectural Forum* magazine, "The Cape Cod was and still is the most efficient house ever developed in America." (Collection of the Levittown Public Library)

NO HYPE. A Type 1 Ranch, which were built along the lines of Frank Lloyd Wright's 1930 Usonian House. The Levitts used their own building techniques as opposed to prefabrication. Alfred's designs also included concealed storage. (Collection of the Levittown Public Library)

NEVER GRADE B, this is a 1951 Type B Ranch, with a thermal-glass living-room window that looked onto the garden and the kitchen in front so moms could carry groceries right in and watch children at play on the front lawn. (Collection of the Levittown Public Library)

A 1951 TYPE 3 RANCH. The last stage of development was the ranch with a finished room in the attic. This model sold for $9,500. The last family, Mr. and Mrs. Ernest Southard, took title on November 19, 1951. Their address was, appropriately, 161 Tardy Lane South. (Collection of the Levittown Public Library)

A 1949 TYPE 2 RANCH. (Collection of the Levittown Public Library)

THE EARLY VET CATCHES THE CAPE. Early Capes, like the ones shown here in 1947, consisted of a kitchen, a 12-by-6-foot living room, two bedrooms, a bathroom, and an unfinished attic. While the early Capes are usually identified as types 1 through 5, depending on slight variation in roof line and window placement, a Levitt brochure identifies the five models as "The Lookout," "The Mariner," "The Snug Harbor," "The Point Pleasant," and "The Green Hills." (Collection of the Levittown Public Library)

A 1949 TYPE 5 RANCH. An October 1949 *Newsday* article "The Utts of Levittown" details the typical cost of living. Al Utt netted $275 a month from both pay and disability checks. Of this, $125 went for food, $64 on house payment, $9 for heating oil, $6.50 for insurance, $5 for telephone, and $15 for time-payments on furniture. Anita Utt said, "That leaves about $40 a month to squander on clothes and recreation." The article also noted that one in every five women was pregnant. (Collection of the Levittown Public Library)

A SOUGHT-AFTER MODEL, a 1949 Type 1 Ranch. The *Newsday* of February 22, 1991, reported that the Smithsonian Institution sought to acquire an unchanged, original ranch or Cape (or both). The Smithsonian staff contacted the Levittown Historical Society to ask that one or two "virgin" homes be donated. So far there has been no donation, most likely because altering, modernizing, and expanding were both necessities and a source of pride among Levittowners. Few homes remain in their original state. (Collection of the Levittown Public Library)

THAT DALTON EYE FOR A PICTURE. A 1950s car took the American dream of the family in the house a step ahead into a car in the carport. Actually, carports, driveways, and garages came later. (Courtesy of Thomas and Beth Dalton)

A WATER TOWER AND CAPE COD HOME. (Courtesy of Thomas and Beth Dalton)

HOPE FOR ALL WHO ENTER. Early families move into their new homes—veritable castles to many. One original Levittowner said she never liked the town or her house from day one, but she stayed anyway. On October 1, 1947, the first three hundred families moved into rental Capes. Mr. and Mrs. Theodore Bladydas moved into "Job No. 1," at 67 Bellmore Road. Cecile Roberts, another early Levittowner, said, "All I needed besides furniture were two fluorescent bulbs and I was all set to move in. It cost me $40 to move. There were no telephone lines—you had to go to a phone box on the corner. My mother, who lived in the Bronx, said that I moved to the end of the earth." (Collection of the Levittown Public Library)

Three

Community Life

"And we're all living here in Allentown" (originally written as Levittown)
—From the song "Allentown" by Billy Joel

"All we had was hope. It was a chance to catch our breath.
It didn't matter who you were or where you came from, but how you lived your life.
Mr. Levitt enabled us to have the good life."
—Levittowner Daphne Rus, in *The Levittown Tribune*, February 4, 1994

In Hofstra University's documentary film on Levittown, created by Professor Stewart Bird and a team of student assistants, Billy Joel neatly synopsized the essence of the place: "It's not as cut-and-dried as people would like to think. It's not as easy as saying, well, it was a cultural wasteland or that it was a boon for GIs. There were a lot of things in the middle . . . There were a lot of different lives being lived. And there were a lot of hopes in that place—a lot of dreams fulfilled and a lot of dreams dashed."

Community life started out with a dichotomy of first-time homeowners and negative aspects including no phones, no trees, and no stores. Retailers drove around Levittown in their station wagons stocked with milk, baby food, and other products. Eventually, Levittown took on a more appealing shape. Levitt built and gave to the community a $250,000 town hall, nine 75-by-100-foot swimming pools valued at $150,000 each, ten parks, including one with a professional-size baseball field and a grandstand, and many playgrounds.

As each hardship was obliterated, however, the restrictive covenant held on despite the popular Jackie Robinson (of the Brooklyn Dodgers), President Truman's integrated armed forces, and the United States Supreme Court ruling that restrictive-housing covenants were unenforceable. Finally, the Levitt company voluntarily accepted minority buyers, and, according to the 1990 Census, the community's racially mixed population of about 54,000 includes blacks, Asians, Hispanics, and others.

From the time that the most frequent question of prospective homeowners was "How soon can we move in?" to the rise of a bustling suburb, life in Levittown evolved light years past condemnations like the one in Robert Goldston's book *Suburbia: Civil Denial*, that described the place as a "proliferating nonentity."

An October 10, 1969 *Newsday* article reported that the "three 'generations' of householders occupy one small part of what was once a one-generation community of World War II veterans. Still young but mature for its twenty-two years, Levittown has what newer developments, notably Commack in Suffolk County, are eagerly seeking—a sense of identity, community pride, participation in local affairs. . . Call it the spirit of Levittown, since it is the result of a unique experience, the group efforts of families in the same age range working together to solve their common problems."

One of these problems was the lack of trees. Initial saplings that didn't survive were replaced by Abraham Levitt, who had an active interest in horticulture and who allegedly knocked on people's doors to find out why their lawn hadn't been mowed or some such neglect. Levitt planted nearly half a million species, including 60,000 fruit trees, 53,000 shade trees, 175,350 evergreens, and 193,000 flowering shrubs. Stores, shops, restaurants, bowling alleys, schools, and houses of worship lent themselves to the families in the more than 17,000 homes built by 1951.

A public library sprang up in 1950, and a fire department in 1954. Other civic and cultural organizations flourished. As Dr. Kelly put it in her article "Learning from Levittown," the Levitt community was "the reduction of the American Dream into an affordable reality." Sociologists as well as the media monitored nearly every aspect of Levittown life, right down to profiling the "ideal" suburban woman, as opposed to the "domestic engineer" image women were fed by magazines and advice columns of the 1920s and '30s.

Dr. Kelly also points out that women of the late 1940s and early '50s were encouraged to be moms/workhorses during the day when hubby was not home, and passive, romantic, and lovely (with the children virtually out of sight) when he was. Oscar Hammerstein II's lyrics to "A Fellow Needs A Girl," a popular song of 1947, instructed that "A fellow needs a girl to sit by his side/At the end of a weary day/To sit by his side and listen to him talk/And agree with the things he'll say." Career-minded women received warning that love would elude them if they chose a career over a husband and children.

The "ideal" suburban man worked all week and then painted or remade furniture or occupied himself with other do-it-yourself projects. A quarterly journal called *Thousand Lanes: Ideas for the Levitt Home* urged them to fix, expand, and remodel whatever they could; lumber yards, hardware stores, painters, and contractors boomed.

Said Clare Worthing to *Newsday* reporter Kenneth Gross: "The wonderful part about Levittown is that when the kids were little, no matter whose house they played in, they all knew where the bathroom was." Mary Heron Quinn, who bought the first Levittown house with her brother Phil (a florist) and sister Adele, added that sometimes kids would saunter into the wrong house altogether because the homes looked so alike. Quinn also recounted that many young Levittown women lost their husbands in the war, and told of the days when she and her family would take the long, long walk to the nearest Catholic church, since they could not afford a car.

During the Blizzard of '47, Quinn said she'd boarded the train to Levittown after standing all day at her Lord & Taylor's job in New York City. "Not one man would give up his seat," she said. "I was so tired that I even asked one man if I could sit down just for a while, and he refused." But now at a youthful eighty-two, Mary Quinn stood at the counter of the family florist shop on Hempstead Turnpike and made no bones about having a great life and good neighbors in the town that sprang up the same year that "flying saucers" first received widespread publicity, Perry Como's "When You Were Sweet Sixteen" sold a million records, and a Bedouin shepherd boy in the Middle East discovered the cave that yielded the Dead Sea Scrolls.

In short, Levittown blossomed even after William Levitt himself left the area to build new communities, and sociologists and the media continue to examine and interpret this phenomenal place.

BUS STOP. The bus stop sign on Wolcott Road directs people to the North Village Green ("green" meaning shopping center). (Collection of the Levittown Public Library)

US ON THE BUS. Early Levittowners tended to be no-car or one-car families, making public transportation extremely important. (Collection of the Levittown Public Library)

WELCOME WAGON. The advent of suburban life drew neighbors into friendships and support systems. "Welcome Wagon ladies" offered thoughtful gifts donated by local merchants to newcomers. Cottage industries such as Avon and Tupperware thrived as housewives lent an ear to door-to-door salespeople and participated in sales "parties." (Collection of the Levittown Public Library)

SAFETY FIRST. The girl riding her bicycle probably had no idea that Levitt's road curves were designed specifically to discourage "lead-footed" drivers. Pat Freund, who grew up in Levittown, recalls the houses all being painted very light pastel shades, and as a little girl, she had the common experience of mistakenly walking into a neighbor's home. (Collection of the Levittown Public Library)

GREETINGS! No draft-notice salutation here, but a joyful family at the door of their new home. (Collection of the Levittown Public Library)

A HOUSE THAT LEVITT BUILT, c. 1952. (Collection of Levittown Public Library)

SUBURBAN SMILE. Estelle Eastwood (Clare Worthing's mother), c. 1949, had her picture taken with a Cape on Cove Lane and a '47 Oldsmobile behind her. (Courtesy of Jerry and Clare Worthing)

A LASSIE'S BEST FRIEND. Joan Worthing and her collie, Buff, stand at the entrance of a neighbor's house, with little Jackie Levy behind the door. A rite of passage for many of the pioneers who were former city dwellers was the acquisition of a family pet. Levitt's ownership agreement even dealt with pets: "The keeping of animals is prohibited except for not more than two domestic animal pets." (Courtesy of Jerry and Clare Worthing)

WASHER WITH GIRL. Joan Worthing was too young to realize that the Bendix washing machine, included in the price of the house, was a luxury to people who previously did their laundry by hand or used laundry services. Ceil Roberts said her Bendix lasted for thirty-two years. The Levitt covenant prohibited hanging wash outdoors on weekends: "Only portable dryers are permitted. They must be used only in the rear yard—not on Saturdays, Sundays or holidays—and removed from the outside when not in use." (Courtesy of Jerry and Clare Worthing)

HOMO SAPIENS "SUBURBUS." Jerry Worthing in 1953 is shown here with his '52 Pontiac. The Worthings could be viewed as the quintessential "Mr. and Mrs. Levittown." The handsome couple grew up in Merrick, Long Island, and met at Jones Beach. During the war, Jerry was a sergeant in the Signal Corps. He became an electrical engineer who completed his education under the GI Bill, and Clare became a model. (Courtesy of Jerry and Clare Worthing)

MR. AND MRS. ABRAHAM LEVITT. Abraham, born July 1, 1880, in Brooklyn, was the son of Russian-born rabbi Louis Levitt and Nellie Levitt, born in Austria-Germany. The family was poor, and Abraham left school at an early age, though eventually he was admitted to New York University Law School. In 1906, he married Pauline Biederman, and they reared two sons, William Jaird and Alfred Stuart. Abraham practiced law until 1929, when he founded the Levitt and Sons firm. In the 1930s, the firm specialized in custom homes in Rockville Centre and Manhasset, Long Island. Abraham was the force behind the philosophy and aesthetic sense that contributed to Levittown as a community. (Collection of Levittown Public Library)

ISLAND TREES SHOPPING GREEN, Hempstead Turnpike, 1949, a precursor of the modern strip-mall. (Collection of Levittown Public Library)

SLATE LANE SWIMMING POOL, one of nine pools built by the Levitts for the community. The other pools were on Carmen Avenue, Levittown Parkway, West Village Green, Azalea Road, East Village Green, North Village Green, South Village Green, and Bluegrass Lane. The pools measured 75-by-150 feet. Anyone brave enough to say he remembers when the plastic bathing cap was required for swimming pool users is a bona fide baby boomer. (Collection of Levittown Public Library)

DANCE, BALLERINA, DANCE! Ballet class was part of Levittown's cultural life for children. (Collection of Levittown Public Library)

CAPES, CAPES, EVERYWHERE, 1947–48. Mary Heron Quinn, her brother Phil, and her sister Adele were the first buyers of a Levittown home. In a recent interview, Mrs. Quinn said, "People today don't appreciate William Levitt. He was a wonderful man. We were living in a two-room apartment in Queens with my mother. When Levitt called to say he had a home for us at 2 Meadow Lane, we jumped at the opportunity and bought it sight unseen." (Collection of Levittown Public Library)

WELCOME TO LEVITTOWN . . . Along with the admonition to drive carefully, the "Welcome to Levittown" sign gives the times of meetings for such important organizations such as the Lions Club (Corte's, 2nd and 4th Tuesdays, 7:30 pm) and the Rotary International (Caruso's Restaurant, Tuesday, 12:10). (Collection of Levittown Public Library)

WATER TOWER. Bikers look tiny in relation to the monstrous structure emblazoned with the town name. (Collection of Levittown Public Library)

IN YOUR EASTER BONNET . . . The Worthings—Jerry, Clare, Joan, and Cathie—pose in front of their '57 Oldsmobile on Easter Sunday, 1960. The carport is the Worthing's; the house in the background is a neighbor's. Jerry and Clare followed the evolution of Levittown from renting a cape, purchasing a ranch, raising a family, and participating in community affairs to retiring and celebrating Levittown's 50th anniversary. (Courtesy of Jerry and Clare Worthing)

A YOUNG WILLIAM JAIRD LEVITT, known eventually as Mr. Levittown.

THE RED APPLE, which later became Caruso's Restaurant, on Hempstead Turnpike. Said Phil Heron, who owned a florist shop a few doors down from Caruso's, "There was no shopping around here except for the old Red Apple Restaurant (now Caruso's). So we'd hitchhike into Hempstead with a shopping list for the people next door." (*The Levittown Tribune*, July 20, 1967.) Caruso's later became Steve's Steak House, followed by the Hollywood Grill, now defunct. (Collection of Levittown Public Library)

GUESS WHO! Billy Joel, who would become the famous singer/songwriter, gives a grin as he sits on the front lawn at 20 Meeting Lane—the Levitt home, Hicksville, he grew up in. (Courtesy of Billy Joel)

CHURCH ROAD HILL. This 1961 Ben Schnell photograph emphasizes one of the few hills in Levittown, a change from the barren landscape of 1947. With the addition of personal touches and mature shrubs, the houses have taken on their own personalities. (Collection of Levittown Public Library)

STREET SCENE, 1957. Ben Schnell snapped a quiet moment in Levittown. (Collection of Levittown Pubic Library)

ON THE WAGON? Four-year-old Joan Worthing pulls her little sister Cathie, age one and a half, while showing off the latest in swimwear. (Courtesy of Jerry and Clare Worthing)

LET IT SNOW! The snow that began to fall on the Friday morning of December 26, 1947, was to become the Blizzard of '47. Before it was over, there were accumulations of 26 inches and drifts of more than 5 feet. Some commuters were stranded in the city, while others trudged part of the way on foot. Many homeowners were caught without shovels. All in all, the "pioneers," who had barely moved in, took the storm in stride and helped each other out. Marion and Harry Bagnaco recalled that parents put the kids to bed and ice-skated in the streets. (Collection of Levittown Public Library)

SNOWMAN. Homeowners could not escape dealing with storms any more than they could escape death and taxes. In this 1950s photograph, the gentleman is fortunate enough to have the benefit of a snowblower. (Collection of Levittown Public Library)

LEVITT IMMORTALIZED. On October 28, 1951, Abraham Levitt was honored with a plaque recognizing his contributions. He stands with the white-haired sculptor, Julio Kilenyi, as Dr. Arthur V. Jason admires the work. A horticulturist by avocation, Levitt landscaped Levittown. A well-known figure, he was often seen in his chauffeur-driven Cadillac checking on plantings. Reports are that he'd as quickly chastise a homeowner for a poorly cared-for lawn as he would have a dying shrub replaced. In 1948, Abraham wrote a weekly column, "Chats on Gardening," for the *Levittown Tribune*. He also wrote the company brochure, "The Care of Your Lawn and Landscaping" and an article in *American Home* magazine, "Fruit is Fine for Little Gardens." (Collection of Levittown Public Library)

SPLIT-RAIL FENCES were all the rage in the 1950s. (Collection of Levittown Public Library)

48

BETTER THAN THE BRECK GIRL. Clare Worthing models in 1948. Clare was active in the school PTA, and she noted that the transition from a rural school system serving fewer than 100 students to the thousands of Levittown students required the large-scale involvement of parents. "Levittown was the most fantastic learning-place for people," said Clare, "especially given that the original (Jerusalem) school district was a three-room schoolhouse." (Courtesy of Jerry and Clare Worthing)

HANGING OUT ON THE HAMMOCK. Joan Worthing (far right) poses with some of her friends. (Courtesy of Jerry and Clare Worthing)

"OUR HOUSE IS A VERY, VERY, VERY FINE HOUSE." This unidentified family stands proudly in front of their ranch, c. 1960s. (Collection of Levittown Public Library)

MAYS' HEYDAY. The department store, Mays, was on Hempstead Turnpike. Today the building is occupied by the Tri-County Flea Market. In the 1940s and '50s, Long Island became known as "the fertile acres" because of its population explosion. The number of young families created a demand for not only housing, but an incredible market for goods and services. (Collection of Levittown Public Library)

IMP AT LARGE. Billy Joel posed for this picture, which was taken looking down Meeting Lane toward Winter Lane. (Courtesy of Billy Joel)

TAKE ME OUT TO THE BALLGAME. Little League coach Frank Casale is surrounded by young helpers recruiting "umps, coaches and managers for the Little League." They are holding copies of the book, *Stan the Man's Hit Record*. On June 22, 1963, Stan Musial broke Ty Cobb's Major League record of 5,800 career bases. (Collection of Levittown Public Library)

SOUTH VILLAGE GREEN SHOPPING CENTER, WHERE ARE YOU? Garden apartments replaced the green. (Collection of Levittown Public Library)

RANCH AMONG THE BRANCHES. The Better Education League of Levittown, an organization that provided support for public education, sponsored house tours as a fund-raising activity. These popular tours gave members of the community the opportunity to see home improvements other owners made. (Collection of Levittown Public Library)

THE JOEL FAMILY. Billy Joel (left) poses in the family backyard with his sister Judy, his maternal grandmother Rebecca Nyman, and his mother, Rosalind Nyman Joel. (Courtesy of Billy Joel)

WE ARE SIAMESE IF YOU PLEASE . . .
Cathie Worthing at age fourteen gets a kick
out of Sami in 1967. Sami obliges the
photographer with an alluring twist of her
head. Cathie works today as a psychotherapist
in Vermont. (Courtesy of Jerry and Clare
Worthing)

A CLASSIC FIRETRUCK. (Collection of Levittown Public Library)

MAN'S BEST FRIEND: Jerry Worthing and Buff in 1950. Beautiful collies were especially loved because of the popular television show *Lassie*, which aired from September 12, 1954, to September 12, 1971. Timmy, her young owner, was portrayed by Tommy Rettig (1954–57), followed by Jon Provost (1957–64). The show received Emmy awards in 1954 and 1955 for Best Children's Program. (Courtesy of Jerry and Clare Worthing)

HOME IMPROVEMENT. The Worthings added a jalousie porch in 1957. Jerry said the design of the Levitt house lent itself to expansion. His home is described in the September 30, 1961 house tour: "A flagstone entrance hall leads into a dramatic home featuring a dining room with a beamed ceiling built in the carport area and an extended living room. Unique handling of upstairs space creates a sophisticated bedroom suite with perfection of detail. Other examples of ingenious space utilization will be found downstairs." (Courtesy of Jerry and Clare Worthing)

LITTLE LANDSCAPER. The little boy with the lawnmower would have been a child after Abraham Levitt's own heart. This 1967 photograph reveals a well-tended front yard, which lives up to a sign mentioned in a *National Geographic* article that predicted Levittown would be a garden spot of the world. This aspect of home ownership was part of the covenant: "Lawns must be cut and tall weeds removed at least once a week between April 15 and Nov. 15." Enforcement of many articles of the covenant gradually faded away. (Collection of Levittown Public Library)

PROM NIGHT. Levittown Memorial High School juniors are all dolled up for their prom in 1958. From left to right are as follows: (sitting) Donna Matthews, Pete Ryan, Freda Bruey, and David DeChester; (standing) Artie Goldhammer, two unidentified prom-goers, and Jeanne Slingo. (Courtesy of Donna Ryan)

LEVITTOWN HALL, a view from the stage, a photograph by William Thomas. The hall, built at a cost of $250,000, has a main room that seats five hundred, along with smaller meeting rooms. The hall houses the plaque by Julio Kilenyi honoring Abraham Levitt. (Collection of Levittown Public Library)

MODEL RAILROADERS. Boys in the 1950s took their Lionel and other trains seriously. It was a hobby that rivaled today's Nintendos and computer games. (Collection of Levittown Public Library)

THE WATERMELON EATERS. Not exactly a model for a painting by Van Gogh, this girl is trying her best in a watermelon-eating contest in Levittown. It might have been the pits. (Collection of Levittown Public Library)

BABY TOURIST AT HAVEN LANE. This photograph by Charles Serge captures part of the 1969 "House Tour of Outstanding Levittown Homes," sponsored by the Better Education League. In the 1960s, Dr. Barbara Kelly of Hofstra University organized walking tours of a different type, however. Levittown was considered "the ultimate suburb" because of its size, affordability, and planned nature and was often the subject of sociological study. On Dr. Kelly's tours, students would see a thriving social experiment. (Collection of Levittown Public Library)

YOU ONLY HAVE TO LOOK IN YOUR OWN BACKYARD. The boy who would grow up to become the famous performer Billy Joel sits at the picnic table with his father, Howard Joel (left), sister Judy, and grandmother Rebecca Nyman. Most likely Billy's mother, Rosalind, snapped the picture. How wonderful that a superstar like Billy Joel would open his family album to share these priceless photos as a celebration of Levittown's 50th anniversary! (Courtesy of Billy Joel)

A DYNAMIC DUO. Joan and Cathie Worthing (eight months old) are shown here in 1954. Today, Joan is a math and computer science teacher at Riverhead High School, Long Island. (Courtesy of Jerry and Clare Worthing)

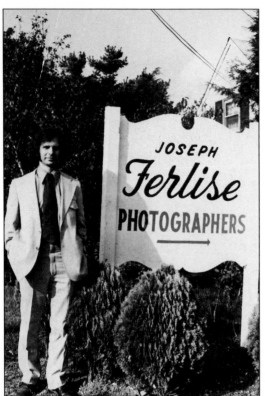

WATCH THE BIRDIE. Joseph Ferlise, an Air Force veteran, bought a Levittown ranch in 1965 and started a business in it. He subsequently bought another house across the street in which to live. Said Ferlise, "This is a tightly knit community. I stayed because I felt my roots were here—it's my home, my family, my people, and it was a big change from military life. The photography business has changed over the years, too, but it was built on repeat customers from the community." Ferlise has two children, Joseph Jr. and Christina, and three step-children: AnneMarie, Christina, and Lisa. (Courtesy of Joseph Ferlise)

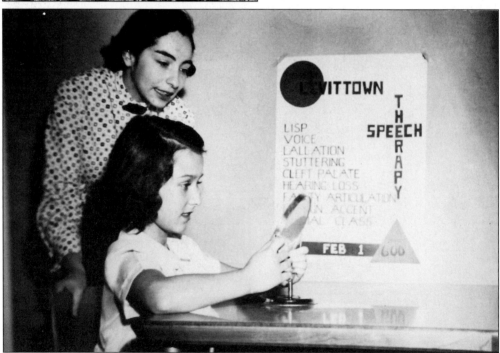

COMMUNITY CAREGIVING. Speech therapy was available through the Levittown community. (Collection of Levittown Public Library)

AH, THE JOYS OF HOME
OWNERSHIP! The lady of the house in
1967 attends to watering. An integral part
of home ownership was the care and
maintenance of the lawn. For many of the
former city-dwellers, the new responsibility
could be alternately a joy, a burden, an ice-
breaker and conversation piece, and a
source of puzzlement (because they didn't
have experience caring for lawns). In the
early days, a lawn that remained uncut
would be cut by Levitt and the bill sent to
the owner. Erma Bombeck, the chronicler
of the suburban experience, satirized the
battle of lawn maintenance in her book
*The Grass is Always Greener Over the Septic
Tank*. (Collection of Levittown Public
Library)

PRINCE ALBERT? The press release for this event read: "The Levittown Public Library
program 'Canning, Preserving and Freezing,' presented by Mrs. Vera Rivers (center) of the
Nassau County Extension Service, included a Tasting Table of home-prepared gourmet foods
donated by library staff, and a recipe book of the taste treats. Above, Mrs. Rivers serves Mrs.
Feldman from the Tasting Table, while Mrs. Helen Crisafulli (left), holding one of the recipe
books, considers her selection." (Collection of Levittown Public Library)

MACLAREN STADIUM. (Collection of Levittown Public Library)

DONATION. Harold Abbott presents a check to two representatives of the Salvation Army. Today, a chapter of the charitable organization is at 148 Gardiners Avenue in Levittown. (Collection of Levittown Public Library)

I LOVE A PARADE. Photographer Steve Kummerman caught the 1967 parade through the Levittown shopping center. Names such as Lobels and the W.T. Grant Co. were part of the era's household references. (Collection of Levittown Public Library)

SQUARE-DANCERS celebrate the 10th anniversary of Levittown in 1957 in front of Mays department store. The E.J. Korvettes story parallels the Levitts' success at the time. David Halberstam wrote in his book, *The Fifties*: "In the summer of 1953, Eugene Ferkauf . . . looked at the potato fields of Westbury and experienced a great vision of the new suburbia: a sparkling, huge new store with vast parking facilities . . ." Ferkauf established E.J. Korvettes, named for Eugene (Ferkauf), Joe Swillenberg, and a mutation of the World War II Canadian subchaser called the Corvette. Because Korvettes blossomed as the Korean War ended, and because the retailers were Jewish, it was erroneously believed that the name stood for "Eight Jewish Korean War Veterans." (Collection of Levittown Public Library)

"STRIKE IT RICH." Emcee Warren Hulls (center), an unidentified man, and Nina Ladoff have a good time at the CBS quiz show, *Strike It Rich*, which aired from 1951 to 1955. Quiz shows such as this and *The $64,000 Question* had a wide audience as watching TV became a great American pastime. Shock waves ran wild when handsome Columbia University professor Charles Van Doren said before a Congressional committee on November 2, 1959, "I was involved . . . in a deception," referring to the cheating on the show *Twenty-One*. (Collection of Levittown Public Library)

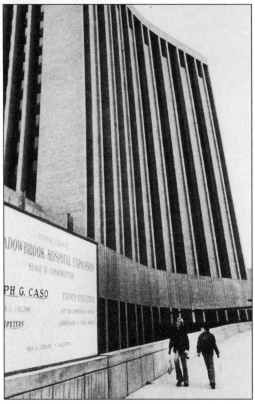

THE NASSAU COUNTY MEDICAL CENTER. (Collection of Levittown Public Library)

THE ORIGINAL DALTON FUNERAL HOME was a farmhouse on Hempstead Turnpike. Today there are five Dalton funeral homes on Long Island. Proprietor Thomas Dalton also published *The Levittowner* newspaper and was active in many civic and charitable activities. (Courtesy of Thomas and Beth Dalton)

RAH, RAH, SIS-BOOM-BAH! The 1952–53 cheerleading squad is shown here with coach Christine Marasa standing in the center. (Collection of Levittown Public Library)

MERCY! The Levittown League for Mercy Hospital holds a membership tea at MacArthur Hall. While Levitt donated land for schools and churches, the "pioneers" invested much "sweat equity" into creating other helping organizations. (Collection of Levittown Public Library)

THE FIRST FERLISE RANCH served as both home and photographic studio on the corner of Jerusalem Avenue and Taylor Lane. (Courtesy of Joseph Ferlise)

JOSEPH FERLISE AND JOSEPH JR. chat during the late 1960s. Ferlise's son works with Dad in the family photography business. "We're with people at the happy times of their life," Ferlise said. (Courtesy of Joseph Ferlise)

LEVITTOWN CHARITY. Salvation Army representatives check the tags of children lined up for an outing. (Collection of Levittown Public Library)

MICHELANGELO WOULD BE PROUD to see this Levitt homeowner sprucing up his shutters in 1967. One of the perennial occupations of Levittowners was improving and individualizing their homes. Businesses ranging from supplying storms windows and screens to the complete finishing of attic rooms sprang up and catered to the needs of homeowners, do-it-yourself or otherwise. With the scarcity of cash of many families and pride of ownership, home improvement was the hobby of choice for the young vets. (Collection of Levittown Public Library)

HAPPY FAMILY. The Worthing family gathered in 1960 behind the Worthing home. Jerry Worthing is at the far left. For many, Levittown was a family affair with brothers, sisters, and cousins buying homes in the same neighborhood. Jerry's father bought a home a few blocks away. Levittowner Pat Freund remembers having two sets of cousins living within a few blocks of each other. Pat's mother moved to Levittown, followed shortly by two brothers and a sister and their families. (Courtesy of Jerry and Clare Worthing)

TEAMWORK. The Levittown Little League was sponsored by Dalton Funeral Home in 1974. (Courtesy of Thomas and Beth Dalton)

OLD CARS parked at the Levittown Drug Center reveal the popularity of the shopping greens. (Courtesy of Joseph Ferlise)

LITTLE PATRIOT. This boy watches a Levittown parade. For a town of veterans, the Memorial Day parade took on great significance. (Collection of Levittown Public Library)

LEVITTOWN'S BRIGHTEST watch a ballgame. (Collection of Levittown Public Library)

PRETTY BARBARA RYAN stands on the lawn of 59 Hill Lane in 1949. The Ryan family photographs capture the daily life of Levittowners. (Courtesy of Donna Ryan)

PATRICK AND PETER RYAN stand in front of the Hill Lane house in 1953. One can't help but notice how the tree filled out since Barbara posed there four years earlier. (Courtesy of Donna Ryan)

ALL SMILES. Peter and Patrick Ryan mug for the camera in the spring of 1949. (Courtesy of Donna Ryan)

AN AMERICAN CAR AS LONG AS THE STREET. A woman steps out of the car in front of St. Bernard's Church, 1960. Dr. Mark's brick house and Mays are across the street, Hempstead Turnpike. (Courtesy of Donna Ryan)

THE ISRAEL COMMUNITY CENTER is "a synagogue center, combining the functions of a synagogue with those of a community center," according to an ICC brochure. Author Albert Gordon quotes Louis Goldberg, one of the first presidents of the synagogue: "It was May 14, 1948. A few of us (six couples) sitting in my living room on that night heard the radio broadcast that Israel had declared itself a nation. We were all excited about that. The men in the room were all ex-GIs. We suddenly decided that we just had to organize a synagogue and center in Levittown, and that we must call it Israel Synagogue Center in honor of the new state of Israel." (Collection of Levittown Public Library)

THE LEVITTOWN FIRE DEPARTMENT was established in 1954. Fire companies of Levittown, Island Trees, East Meadow, Wantagh, and North Bellmore serve the area. (Collection of Levittown Public Library)

AWARD WINNER Thomas F. Dalton (left) accepts a plaque acknowledging his contributions as president of the Levittown Chamber of Commerce. Donald Rule presents the award as Father Ballweg looks on approvingly. (Courtesy of Thomas and Beth Dalton)

TOUCHDOWN! The first varsity football team of Levittown High School play in 1953 on what is now the site of the Division Avenue High School. (Collection of Levittown Public Library)

74

IN THE SPIRIT. Levittowners pose behind the holiday greeting from the Levittown Chamber of Commerce. (Courtesy of Joseph Ferlise)

FUTURE SLAMDUNKERS. The Levittown High School freshman basketball team gathers for a photograph in 1952. The coach is John Lenz. (Collection of Levittown Public Library)

PUNCH AND JUDY. A puppet show delights children. The Levittown library sponsored a wide variety of educational and cultural programs. In the summer of 1970, the library began sponsoring performances by the Nassau County Puppet Mobile in Veterans Memorial Park. Children's librarian Susan Messer holds three-year-old Lori Pediman, while Vincent Michaelis, director of Active Parks in Nassau County, holds two-year-old Steve Hodel. Karen Elicati has her arms full of books. (Collection of Levittown Public Library)

LEVITTOWN LIBRARIAN Cecile J. Roberts reads to youngsters in 1953. After forty-three years of service, Mrs. Roberts retired in 1993 but still worked two mornings a week, said director Peter Martin. One of her most outstanding accomplishments was her work as the library's coordinator for the Senior Connection, a cooperative county-wide self-help program for seniors. (Collection of Levittown Public Library)

THE ZINO CONSTRUCTION CO., INC. started in 1952 in the garage of Ben Zino's home on Mansfield Avenue in Levittown. It would grow into the largest construction company on Long Island. "I started . . . with a telephone and a traveling hammer," said Zino in a local newspaper article citing Levittown's 40th anniversary. "The big business back then was creating a third bedroom where the attic was." By 1987, Zino's staff grew from three to more than one hundred. (A Ferlise Photo, courtesy of Joseph Ferlise)

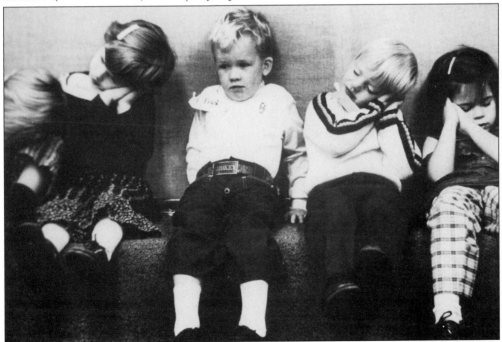

LULLABYE. Of these unidentified toddlers, only Erich remains awake. (Collection of Levittown Public Library)

THE CIRCLE M RANCH TEAM, Northern Levittown Little League, in an early photo. (Collection of Levittown Public Library)

THE CENTRAL LEAGUE TEAM, Levittown Little League, sponsored by Kenien Lumber in 1968. (Collection of Levittown Public Library)

HERE WE COME A-WASSAILING. Neighborhood Christmas carolers gather in December 1963. (Courtesy of Jerry and Clare Worthing)

THE 1952 LITTLE LEAGUE CHAMPIONS. Manager Bob Hudson and commissioner Hugh Jock present a trophy. (Collection of Levittown Public Library)

THE ESSO STATION is located next to the Meenan Oil Company, which provided home heating oil, in Hempstead. The company moved to Wantagh and still serves Levittown homes. (Collection of Levittown Public Library)

THEY LIKE IKE. The Levittown Republican Club, c. 1950. (Collection of Levittown Public Library)

THE POSTMAN'S APPOINTED ROUNDS. Levittown celebrates as it acquires its own post office in the 1950s. (Collection of Levittown Public Library)

BENEDICTION is given at the post office opening day by Rabbi Herman Grossman. (Collection of Levittown Public Library)

THE PLEDGE OF ALLEGIANCE is recited at the post office opening celebration. (Collection of Levittown Public Library)

THE GRADUATES of sixth grade in 1963 gather on Weaving Lane to have their picture taken. (Courtesy of Jerry and Clare Worthing)

A LIVING ROOM of a Levitt home on Bluegrass Lane and Hempstead Turnpike. (Collection of Levittown Public Library)

A WORTHY INTERIOR. This "cubbyhole," added by Jerry and Clare Worthing, was featured in *Woman's Day* magazine as a perfect place for the telephone, a comfy seat, and decorative storage. (Courtesy of Jerry and Clare Worthing)

THE LIVING AND DINING area of a Levitt home. (Collection of Levittown Public Library)

A COZY DINING ROOM, c. 1950s. (Collection of Levittown Public Library)

EVERYONE LIKES THE KITCHEN BEST. Kitchens came complete with G.E. refrigerators and electric stoves, Tracey cabinets, stainless steel sinks, and the Bendix washer were neatly tucked away to maximize the use of space. (Collection of Levittown Public Library)

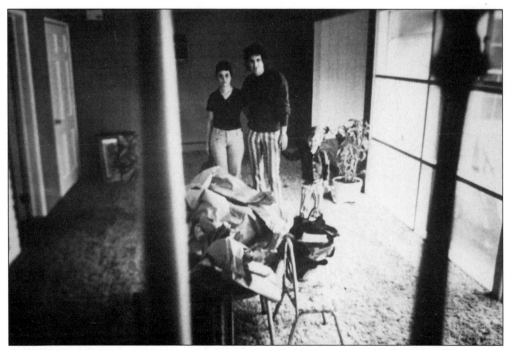

A YOUNG FAMILY, c. 1960s, stands in an expanded living room. (Collection of Levittown Public Library)

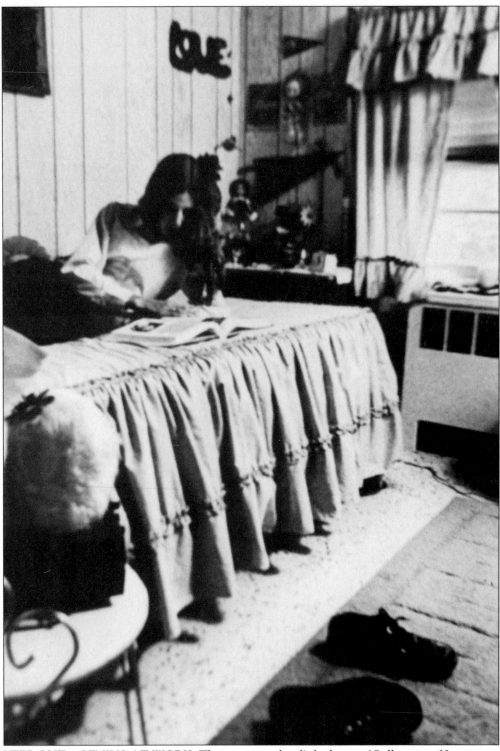

KEEP OUT—GENIUS AT WORK. This is a typical girl's bedroom. (Collection of Levittown Public Library)

THE INTERIOR of one of the homes featured in the Levittown house tours shows the elaborate changes some owners made to the basic Levitt home. (Collection of Levittown Public Library)

THE HOUSE AT 87 WEAVING LANE boasts a lovely living/dining area. This photograph was taken by R & S Naskin. (Collection of Levittown Public Library)

MR. SUCCESS, William Levitt, at the Lake Success company headquarters. Eric Larrabee, writing for *Harper*'s magazine, unkindly described Levitt as "a retired Marx brother turned master-of-ceremonies in a run-down nightclub." Throughout his life, Levitt evoked strong sentiments, both positive and negative. Fact is, he was a legend and did not plead perfection. (Collection of Levittown Public Library)

Four

Schools, Churches, and the Library

"There is only one thing that can kill the Movies, and that is education."
—Will Rogers, 1949

"Little minds are interested in the extraordinary; great minds in the commonplace."
—Elbert Hubbard, 1911

True to his promise to create neighborhoods rather than developments, William Levitt watched Levittown's young families mushroom. Parents joined the PTA, school boards, churches, and synagogues, and became Friends of the Library, which provided many activities and services such as its bookmobiles.

In 1947, Island Trees had a population of 450; its school district had one three-room school with 47 pupils and 2 teachers. By 1968, the population hit nearly 60,000, and there were 11 elementary schools, 3 junior high and 3 senior high schools, and 950 teachers.

Many residents described a special feeling of camaraderie as playpens and high-chairs were passed along, kids entered school, and lawns and train schedules were topics for commiseration. Three denominations—Catholics, Jews, and Protestants—in the first years of Levittown all were anxious to develop their own houses of worship. Papers such as *Thousand Lanes* and *The Levittowner* focused on concerns of the community. One aspect of ownership of a Levitt home that has been criticized was the covenant, which homeowners signed. Some of the terms they agreed to were not to hang wash on weekends, to keep lawns mowed, and not to erect fences. The exclusionary clauses of the covenant were later declared unconstitutional. Sociologists claimed people's freedom of choice and individuality were compromised by regimenting what people were to do on their own property. Gans, who studied Willingboro, a Levitt community in New Jersey, felt the rules initially represented lifestyle choices willingly made by residents.

SCHOOL ANNEX. A Quonset hut in 1948 on Wisdom Lane served as one of Levittown's first schools. Quonset was the trade name of prefabricated huts made of semi-circular sheets of metal to form the walls. (Collection of Levittown Public Library)

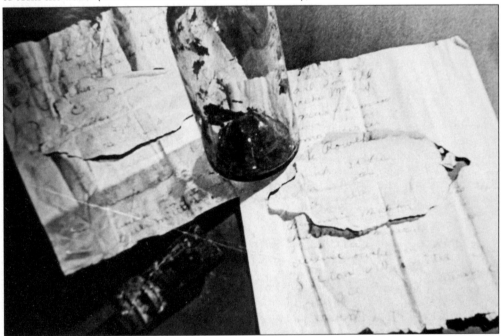

TIME IN A BOTTLE. A bottle from Island Trees School was a "time capsule" left by the class of 1906. It was found in 1970, unearthed beneath a tree taken down in preparation for a shopping center. The tree had been planted in an Arbor Day commemoration. The bottle contained a message signed by twenty-eight students and their teacher, William Peake, along with a poem on beauty written in Latin by scholarly local resident Noble Heath. The message translated: "We shall be made great through unceasing virtue, courage and also truth. We shall always strive for the sky, the planets and the stars. We shall love beauty forever." (Collection of Levittown Public Library)

ISLAND TREES SCHOOL was the only school in existence when Levitt began building. Surviving class members Michael Francis Stokes and Birdsall Sparke remembered that the school was heated by a coal stove, grades were divided by rows, and the annual teacher's salary was $400. Built in 1903, the school was considered a landmark when it was destroyed by fire in 1953. (Collection of Levittown Public Library)

ABBEY LANE SCHOOL, soon after construction. (Collection of Levittown Public Library)

ABBEY LANE SCHOOL, in a later photograph, shows trees and shrubbery and a later model car. Principal Dr. Rose Auteri noted that in 1991–92, the school was given the Academic State School Award of Excellence. It was one of only five schools in the state to receive this honor. (Collection of Levittown Public Library)

WHEELS. St. Bernard School in 1967 shows the transportation of choice—the two-wheeler. The school was erected in 1960. One can even see a relic from the past, the infamous "banana seat." (Collection of Levittown Public Library)

THE JONAS E. SALK MIDDLE SCHOOL, pictured here in 1969. In 1942–53, Americans faced an enemy of a different sort from the problems bequeathed by the war: the polio epidemic. In 1950, 33,000 cases of infantile paralysis were reported. Named for the scientist who developed the Salk vaccine, which virtually eradicated the disease by the 1960s, the school opened in 1957–58 as a high school. When the General MacArthur High School opened in 1960, the Salk school became a junior high with its own little theater and a Get-It-Together program for students experiencing difficulties. (Collection of Levittown Public Library)

ONLY GOD CAN MAKE A TREE. Scouts plant a tree at Memorial High School. (Collection of Levittown Public Library)

LET THE GAMES BEGIN. Children play in 1969 at the Cherrywood Elementary School. (Collection of Levittown Public Library)

THE GENERAL DOUGLAS MACARTHUR HIGH SCHOOL on Old Jerusalem Road. (Collection of Levittown Public Library)

THE FIRST RECITAL, in 1950, of the Levittown School Dancing Program. (Collection of Levittown Public Library)

STOP. Boys on the bikes set an example of safety for other youths. In an effort to increase safety, Levitt designed the curvilinear streets, which reduced four-way stops. (Collection of Levittown Public Library)

ALFRED STUART LEVITT's architectural prowess played an integral part in the success of the Levitt and Sons firm. Halberstam wrote: "By the time of their third Levittown, Abraham had retired, and Alfred, unable to get along with his brother, had sold his shares of stock and gotten out of the company." The 1961–65 edition of *The Dictionary of American Biography* reports that "although most of the publicity . . . focused on William's role, (Abraham) Levitt maintained that William would not have succeeded without Alfred nor Alfred without William." Alfred died of a heart attack in 1966, at age fifty-four. He was survived by his wife, four sons, two daughters, and two grandchildren. (Collection of Levittown Public Library)

THE CIRCULATION DESK at the old Levittown Public Library. (Collection of Levittown Public Library)

BATON TWIRLERS practice their skill at a Levittown event. (Collection of Levittown Public Library)

A GOLF TROPHY is presented. Pictured are Thomas Dalton (left) and Bud King of the parks department. The third man is unidentified. (Courtesy of Thomas and Beth Dalton)

GIRL SCOUTS, members of an increasingly popular American organization that taught love of God and country, are commended. (Collection of Levittown Public Library)

THE DIVISION AVENUE HIGH SCHOOL was the subject of a November 7, 1959 article in *Businessweek*, "Training Ground for Technicians," which examined the vocational program. This was an outgrowth of the 1958 National Defense Education Act that authorized the spending of $15 million per year to help states expand vocational education. A $50,000 federal grant funded the school's electronics laboratory. (Collection of Levittown Public Library)

THE OLD LEVITTOWN PUBLIC LIBRARY with bookmobile parked in front, 1953. The library began in 1950 in rented stores in the South Village Green. Initially, the bookmobile provided services to 1,300 children. The service was so well received that by 1958, the library purchased a second bookmobile at $20,000. In that year alone, the bookmobile circulated 124,500 books. (Collection of Levittown Public Library)

RUTH MILLER was a dedicated professional, an early proponent of the bookmobile service, and the first director of Levittown Public Library. The photograph was taken by D.D. Spellman of Detroit. (Collection of Levittown Public Library)

SATURDAY MORNING STORY TIME, 1957, with librarian Martha Dykes. (Collection of Levittown Public Library)

THE BOOKMOBILE. The young man in the center seems to be an avid reader. In early Levittown, the library and its bookmobiles were controversial because they were paid for out of the school budget. Some residents believed the services were necessary, while others thought them unwarranted and even formed committees for common sense to defeat the expenditure. (Collection of Levittown Public Library)

A HAPPY HALLOWEEN reading group at the library. Levittowners who grew up knowing the benefits and pleasures of the New York Public Library felt the local library was very important. As one resident said, "I can't imagine not having the library." (Collection of Levittown Public Library)

A VERY YOUNG READER in 1951 peruses a picture book in the then double-store library. The library seemed to be an immediate success. The January 1953 Library Bulletin reported that in its first 10 months of operation, 100,000 books had circulated, nearly 10,000 men, women, and children had joined the library, and the original 3,000 volumes had increased to 15,000. (Collection of Levittown Public Library)

A MAN HOLDING A BOOKMOBILE MIRROR. (Collection of Levittown Public Library)

THE FRIENDS OF THE LIBRARY, October 1951. In the early days of the library, when the budget was in danger of being voted down, the Friends rallied support in the community by calling people and asking them to vote for the budget. (Collection of Levittown Public Library)

THE HAUNTED HOUSE READING CLUB. In 1973, the theme for the summer reading club was "The Haunted House." Children's librarian Catherine Romanelli accepts registrations from ten-year-old Sean Delaney (left), seven-year-old Deirdre Pope (center), and six-year-old Kimberly Evans. (Collection of Levittown Public Library)

BELOVED LIBRARIAN CECILE J. ROBERTS exemplified many of the ideal Levittown values, including education and cultural pursuits. A political science graduate of Hunter College, Mrs. Roberts earned an M.S. in library science at the C.W. Post campus of Long Island University. A Manhattan-born woman of many interests, including photography and Frank Lloyd Wright architecture, she was fun-loving, articulate, and unassuming, and contributed to the life of the Levittown library for more than forty-three years. Levittown mourned her death on July 22, 1996. (Courtesy of Levittown Public Library)

FOLK MUSIC AT THE LIBRARY. In May 1969, Naomi Kimmelfield (center) and Joel Loewy (left) presented an evening of folk music. The two teenagers in the back are Randall Sheehi and Lyn Orlowitz. The other boy is unidentified. (Collection of Levittown Public Library)

FIRE! On June 30, 1972, a fire of unknown origin damaged the library's basement storage area and destroyed many seasonal displays made by Jean DeMeglio. The Levittown Fire Department quelled the blaze. (Collection of Levittown Public Library)

STUDENT STEVE PICO holds a poster celebrating the reinstatement of banned books. In February 1976, a board member of an Island Trees school attended a conference that recommended banning certain books. Among them were books written by Kurt Vonnegut, Alice Childress, and Perry Thomas. The member had the books removed from school libraries. Pico took the case to court as a violation of First Amendment rights and won. (Collection of Cecile J. Roberts)

AUTHOR ALICE CHILDRESS AND NATHAN CHILDRESS at the banned-book reinstatement party. (Collection of Cecile J. Roberts)

AUTHOR KURT VONNEGUT AND MRS. JILL KREMINS also attended the reinstatement party on Halloween. (Collection of Cecile J. Roberts)

THE WAY WE WERE. In the late 1950s and early '60s, the community began to experience difficulties with teenagers loitering at the village greens. In 1964, the Youth Direction Council was founded in an effort to address the needs of these young people. James Edmondson, an extremely popular recreation director, was drafted as the council's first director. The council later became known as the Yours, Ours and Mine (YOM) Community Center, Inc. A trailer served as temporary quarters in 1987. (Courtesy of YOM)

YOM FOR KIDS. Ricky Santiago (left), now a supervisor for New York Telephone, and Tom Ashley, now a school principal, ham it up with kids under the YOM sign. (Courtesy of YOM)

YOM PARADERS display their banner in the 1994 Levittown Memorial Day Parade. (Courtesy of YOM)

AMERICAN LEGION MAJOR JOHN KILBRIGHT (left), with Town Presiding Supervisor Joseph Mondello (second from left) honor Friderika Conway, the first woman president of YOM, and James Edmondson, YOM's director. (Courtesy of YOM)

O TANNENBAUM. YOM members Vera Farela (left) and Pauline Hunter served as kitchen aides for seniors. (Courtesy of YOM)

JAMES EDMONDSON (center) receives a check from the Friends of the Library in 1969 to support the youth center. Initially, YOM met with financial problems and skepticism within the community. Edmondson said, "I never thought it wouldn't work." (Courtesy of YOM)

A COMMITTEE FOSTERING LEVITTOWN PRIDE in March 1982 promoted artwork, landscaping, and other aesthetics. One student, third from the left, won a poster contest. County executive Tom Gullotta stands third from right, next to Flo Cullen, co-chair of the committee. Co-chair Joseph Ferlise is second from left, and the unidentified men are from the school district. (Courtesy of Joseph Ferlise)

The Growth of a Parish

Father Daniel J. Martin

THE GROWTH OF A PARISH. Pictured is Father Daniel J. Martin, the pastor of St. Bernard's Church. The first Mass was celebrated on November 7, 1948, by Msr. Thomas O'Brien in a hangar converted into a church. A farmhouse became the rectory. Records note that the number of baptisms was "unbelievably high that year." On May 31, 1970, a fire destroyed St. Bernard's. Pat Freund remembers standing with a group of teenagers on the median on Hempstead Turnpike and crying as they watched the church burn. A new church was built on the foundation and dedicated in 1971. Ten years later, the church was razed after being condemned for structural flaws. Yet another church was built in 1985 that no longer faces Hempstead Turnpike. (Courtesy of Thomas and Beth Dalton)

THE ST. FRANCIS Episcopal Church,
built on an irregular lot donated by Levitt,
makes a pretty picture. (Collection of
Levittown Public Library)

BOY SCOUTS are presented in 1959 at St. Francis Church. From left to right are Augustus
Norton, Thomas Bechman, Gus Norton, Father Maties, David Brown, Ed Kibble, and William
Brown. (Collection of Levittown Public Library)

BLESS THE BEASTS. A pet blessing is held at St. Francis Church. According to church historian and early resident Polly Dwyer, St. Francis has recently celebrated its 26th blessing of the pets. (Collection of Levittown Public Library)

Five

Post-Levitt Communities

"I'm upside down, my head is turning around, I had to leave a little girl in Levittown."
—Allan Sherman, to the tune of "Kingston Town,"
in his 1962 record album, *My Son, the Folk Singer*

The "spinoff" is perhaps best known through television shows: one character shines beyond the script and ends up in a show of his or her own. Levitt's new suburb idea took off like wildfire, and housing developments cropped up all over America (and later in Europe and the Middle East). Writer David Halberstam points out that the multiple Levittowns seemed to embrace TV sitcoms' all-American families, such as the Nelsons and the Cleavers, who were one-income, two-children, two-hot-meals-a-day virtuous families just like the families throughout the neighborhood, although the audience never knew from what states these families hailed or what Ward Cleaver did for a living except that he wore a suit and tie. In sum, they were myths that provided across-the-board models for both family and community life in the 1950s.

"'Spinoff' Levittown, Pa., emerged in 1952," said third-generation Pennsylvania Levittowner George Douglas, an affable, young computer programmer who stopped tending his lawn in order to give us two wayward authors a tour of his later-model Levitt home, the "Country Clubber." "Levitt gave people who otherwise couldn't afford a home a little piece of America," said Douglas. "My grandparents bought a Levitt home in Pennsylvania—humble beginnings. But now these homes are going for $140,000 and more. And I'm really happy here."

Levitt homes also mushroomed and made people happy in Monmouth County, New Jersey, namely in the Strathmore developments in Aberdeen and Marlboro. International Levitt communities eventually sprang up, testimony to the fact that a well-built house is truly a castle.

A PRE-LEVITT FARMHOUSE in Willingboro Township, New Jersey. Once again, in 1958, Levitt's third development transformed a rural community. It was originally called—you guessed it—Levittown, but residents petitioned to have it renamed to its original Willingboro. (Collection of Willingboro Public Library)

PEOPLE SWARMING TO SEE LEVITT MODELS in Willingboro. Levitt recreated his phenomenal success in 1958. There were three models: the ranch, the cape, and colonial, ranging in price from $11,500 to $14,500. On the advice of his wife Rhoda, he alternated the models on the streets. The town became the subject of a sociological study by participant/observer Herbert J. Gans, who lived in the community for two years and took a far kinder view of it than did Lewis Mumford. Gans felt the community was successful because residents shared common values. (Collection of Willingboro Public Library)

AHOY! Part of the challenge of suburban life, except for those lucky enough to work there, has been commuting. The Willingboro commuter boat looks like a pleasant form of travel. (Collection of Willingboro Public Library)

COMEDIAN JACK BENNY golfing at Willingboro Country Club, and possibly celebrating his, uh, 39th birthday, was renowned for feigning miserliness and a lack of ability on violin, for his TV show, and for faking a thirteen-year feud with radio star Fred Allen. The man on the left is unidentified. (Collection of Willingboro Public Library)

A LEVITTOWNER IN P.A. George Douglas, a computer programmer, grew up in Levittown (Bucks County), Pennsylvania, and liked it so much he bought his own home there. George is pictured next to a "Country Clubber" model on Snowball Lane. This model, the largest and most expensive built by Levitt, was originally priced at $17,500. George grew up in a "Levittowner," one of the smallest models, and said his parents enlarged it to three times its original size. (Photo by Tova Navarra)

A "LEVITTOWNER" MODEL in Levittown, Pa., a community begun in 1952. By the time Levitt completed building in Bucks County, there would be 17,311 homes. A one-story model with an original price tag of $9,900 is shown here. In Pennsylvania, Levitt segregated the sections by model rather than alternating models on each street, as in Willingboro. (Photo by Tova Navarra)

MR. GROSS' HOME ON CRABTREE LANE, Levittown, Pa., is a "Rancher" model, originally priced at $8,900. The homes were built with a choice of roof and an unfinished attic. Mr. Gross, the original owner, said he had to put $100 down, later refunded, and added that the home was a great deal for veterans like him. (Photo by Tova Navarra)

A "JUBILEE" model in Levittown, Pa. The "Jubilee" looks remarkably similar to the original Capes in Long Island and sold for $10,990. Two models not pictured are the "Pennsylvanian" and the "Colonial," which sold for $14,500. They were next in size to the "Country Clubber." (Photo by Tova Navarra)

STRATHMORE, a Levitt community in Aberdeen, New Jersey, was built in the early 1960s. This three-bedroom Colonial is where author Margaret L. Ferrer lived for thirteen years. The experience led to her fascination with Levitt communities, hence the inspiration for this book. (Collection of Margaret Ferrer)

A STRATHMORE CAPE in Aberdeen, NJ, shows slight changes with a small porch area and garage. The Strathmore community was sectioned alphabetically, with A, B, C, etc., sections. (Photo by Tova Navarra)

JERRY AND CLARE WORTHING in front of their home, next to the beautiful copper beech tree in 1996. Perhaps their feelings are best summarized in a statement Jerry made during an interview by *Newsday* on July 9, 1971. When asked why the couple continued to live in Levittown, Jerry said: "Call it inverse snobbism. Some people look down on Levittown. But that just means phonies won't live here." He said he and Clare had looked at homes elsewhere, but "nothing I've seen can match this. The people are nice here. The house is nice. You can't get a better value." (Photo by Tova Navarra)

THE CONSTELLATION ROAD HOUSE in Levittown (Long Island) shows extensive, creative renovation and remodeling that abounds in the original Levittown. Cecile J. Roberts said of the modern community, "There is more individuality in style than you would suspect— Colonial next to Moroccan next to Chinese. My house was the worst model of all and held up for forty-eight years because it was so solidly built." (Collection of Cecile J. Roberts)

Six

Fifty Years Later

"I dreamed one night that Peggy and I were at the home of a 30-ish, dark-haired,
exotic-looking woman and an older man, to whom we were saying goodbye.
The woman wept and hugged us, begging us not to leave.
When the man bent down to hug me, he chuckled in a very pleased, grandfatherly way.
I didn't realize until I woke up that the man was William Levitt.
The woman's identity eluded me until a Levittown librarian
dredged up a newspaper photo neither Peggy nor I had seen during our research for this book.
Pictured was Levitt and his third wife, Simone—dark and exotic, the woman in my dream.
Peg and I nearly keeled over. Maybe Bill inspired and is 'supervising' this book from beyond."
—Tova Navarra, 1996

People are forever interested in "where-are-they-now?" columns, probably for the same reasons (inveterate nosiness, among them) that make history exciting. We all seem to enjoy a good evolution. If you ask what happened to the Levittown of fifty years ago, you'll be happy to know it's still right where Bill Levitt and his family put it—and competently holding its own.

The New York Times, Newsday, and other publications faithfully covered Levittown's notable anniversaries, each time saying in various ways that the Long Island community might be favorably compared with today's active, vivacious senior citizens. Upon turning fifty, along with many baby boomers born in 1947, Levittown may have one or two gray hairs but shows no sign of demise or even slowing down.

Levitt homes originally priced at around $8,000 are now being sold for $120,000 and more, according to John Gilbert of Corriston Real Estate Agency. Most of them have been improved and expanded as Levitt encouraged through his architectural strategy, although reports are that most of the original radiant heating systems and copper plumbing pipes are still ship-shape. The landscaping has matured, giving the community of a thousand lanes a wizened, welcoming look to contrast with its former sapling appearance. Main roads including Hempstead Turnpike and Jerusalem Avenue are laden with cars and trucks and traffic. The Mays department store building is now the Tri-County Flea Market, and malls, chain restaurants, and other businesses abound. As songwriter Paul Simon might put it, Levittown is "still crazy after all these years."

One can almost hear Bill Levitt saying, "See? Was I right? Of course I was right."

In fact, he was so right that Levitt communities now exist in Israel, Puerto Rico, India, Spain, Germany, and throughout the United States. The Levittown in Mesnil-St. Denis, France, as reported in *The New York Times* of June 18, 1972, is called the "Residence du Chateau," and consists of six hundred homes built starting in 1966 just outside Versailles. There were five Levitt developments around Paris in 1972, and plans for more. New Levitt homes then cost between $30,000 and $60,000. Andrew L. Lorant, president of Levitt France, told the *Times*, "Bill Levitt used to say, 'People are the same the world over!" If nothing else, the Levitts understood the fundamental human need for shelter and how to deliver a quality product that pleased most of the people most of the time.

YOM AS IT IS NOW. YOM has expanded to meet the changing needs of community members across the lifespan. Today, there is a James A. Edmondson Nursery School, a ten-week summer child-care program, and before- and after-school programs including recreation, counseling, tutoring, and employment services. For senior citizens, there is a Senior Community Service Center, which includes a lunch program, health screenings, caregiver support groups, and socialization activities, and adult daycare for the frail elderly. (Photo by Tova Navarra)

PERFORMER BILLY JOEL in a 1990 photograph by Mark Hannauer. The former Hicksville, Long Island, boy is famous for songs including "Piano Man," "Honesty," "She's Always a Woman to Me," and many others. (Courtesy of Maritime Music, Inc.)

THE "EASTER BUNNY HOUSE," as the authors call it, is an original Levittown Cape with new bay windows and decorations to match every season and holiday. The owner is Peggy Nizinski, who has lived at 32 Salem Lane for thirty-five years. (Photo by Tova Navarra)

FERLISE PHOTOGRAPHERS in 1996 has taken on almost a Californian facade and landscaping, an especially attractive renovation of a Levitt ranch. (Courtesy of Joseph Ferlise)

AN IMPRESSIVE RENOVATION has been made to a home on Bluegrass Lane by expanding the second story. Several years ago, owners with homes that were unaltered were encouraged to apply for landmark status, but there are few of them. (Photo by Tova Navarra)

MURAL, MURAL ON THE WALL. The literary classics mural in the Levittown library's adult reading room is the work of artist/teacher Stanley Kaplan. The mural, carved in Phillipine mahogany, was completed in 1959, and was originally in Levittown Memorial High School. When Memorial was closed in 1984, the mural was moved to the library at the request of the junior and senior classes. The five panels depict *Beowulf*, *The Canterbury Tales*, *Macbeth*, *A Tale of Two Cities*, and *The Scarlet Letter/The Raven*. (Collection of Cecile J. Roberts)

MARY HERON QUINN, one of the purchasers of the first house in Levittown, holds a copy of a *Levittown Tribune* article and photo of her siblings Phil and Adele with Bill Levitt. Mary was working in New York City the day Levitt called the Herons and told them to come right down and sign the contract. Fifty years later, Mary works at Flowers By Phil. Levittown is as much about dreams as it is about houses. If there are a thousand lanes, there must be many thousands of dreams. One of Phil Heron's dreams was his florist shop, where he worked until his death in 1988. The shop lives on, like Levitt's legend. (Photo by Tova Navarra)

Bibliography

Barmash, Isadore. *More than they Bargained for: The Rise and Fall of Korvettes*. New York: Lebhar-Friedman Books/Chain Store Publishing Corp., 1981.

Conrad, Pam. *Our House: The Stories of Levittown*. New York: Scholastic, Inc., 1995.

Dexter, Betsy. *You Must Remember This: 1947*. New York: Warner Books, 1995.

Gans, Herbert J. *The Levittowners: Ways of Life and Politics in a New Suburban Community*. New York: Pantheon Books, 1967.

Gordon, Albert I. *Jews in Suburbia*. Boston: Beacon Press, 1959.

Halberstam, David. *The Fifties*. New York: Villard Books, 1993.

Kaufman, Michael T. "Tough times for Mr. Levittown." *The New York Times* (September 24, 1989.)

Kelly, Barbara M. *Suburbia Re-examined*. New York: Greenwood Press, 1989.

_____. *Expanding the American Dream: Building and Rebuilding Levittown*. New York: State University of New York Press, 1993.

_____, ed. *Long Island: The Suburban Experience*. Heart of the Lakes Publishing, Interlaken, N.Y., 1990.

Kleinfelder, Rita Lang. *When We Were Young: A Baby-Boomer Yearbook*. New York: Prentice Hall General Reference, 1993.

Lewis, Jeanne. "Jerusalem Remembered." *Levittown Tribune* (January 31, 1980.)

Masotti, Louis H., and Jeffrey K. Hadden., eds. *Suburbia in Transition, A New York Times Book*. New York: Franklin Watts, Inc., 1974.

Matarrese, Lynne. "Levittown's Historic Raceway Site." *Long Island Forum* (Fall 1994.)

Mumford, Lewis. *The City in History: Its Origins, Its Transformations, and Its Prospects*. New York: Harcourt, Brace & World, Inc., 1961.

Smits, Edward J. "Nassau Suburbia, U.S.A." Syosset, N.Y.: Friends of the Nassau County Museum, 1974, p. 174.

Spagnoli, Joseph E. *Levittown, N.Y.: An Annotated Bibliography, 1947 to 1972*. Prepared for the Levittown Public Library.